THE BALANCE OF REFLECTION

ROBERT ANTILL

authorHOUSE

AuthorHouse™ UK
1663 Liberty Drive
Bloomington, IN 47403 USA
www.authorhouse.co.uk
Phone: UK TFN: 0800 0148641 (Toll Free inside the UK)
UK Local: 02036 956322 (+44 20 3695 6322 from outside the UK)

Published by AuthorHouse 08/05/2021

ISBN: 978-1-6655-9191-1 (sc)
ISBN: 978-1-6655-9190-4 (e)

THE WAY OF THE HERB

It works like this.

As I have purple as the outside band of my iris nearest the "white" of my eyes i am a purple man therefore i have purple, green and orange in my iris . Therefore i only want and need to smoke purple, green or orange tricloned marijuana. The purple makes me strong and feel strong the green makes me relax and the orange makes me lovely. If you have blue as the outside band of your iris and you are male then you should only smoke and you will need to; blue, yellow or red tricloned marijuana. The blue would make you feel strength and be strong, the yellow would make you feel relaxed and the red would make you feel lovely. If you have green as the outside band of your iris and you are male then you will need to smoke green, orange or purple tricloned marijuana. The green will make you feel and be strong,the orange will make you feel relaxed and the purple will make you fell lovely. If you have yellow as the outside band of your iris and you are male then you will want and need to smoke yellow, blue or red tricloned marijuana. The yellow will make you feel strength and be strong,The blue will make you feel relaxed and the red will make you feel lovely. If you have orange as the outside band of your iris and you are male then you will need and want to smoke orange, purple or green marijuana. The orange will give you strength and feel strong the purple will make you feel relaxed and the green will make you feel lovely. If you have red as the outside band of your iris and you are male then you will want and need to smoke red blue or yellow tricloned marijuana. The red will make you strong and feel strength, the blue will make you relaxed and the yellow will make you feel lovely.

It is important to use only the marijuana with triclones(hairs on the flower)of the three colours in your eyes. marijuana is a spiritual herb. It causes spirit voices in your mind. These voices are not malicious but they are there to guide you to beauty. Do as the voice or voices say or try to understand what they are trying to tell you. They are the spirit voices of people who suffer more than you who need your help. If you ignore them then they will not be helped and will not be able to help you. It is not wrong to converse with them. But do not converse with them with your vocal voice as you will not be able hear them easily! you can converse with them with your minds voice but you will need absolute peace to hear them and to deal with them.

Robert Antill

THE WAY OF THE HASHISH

I think women should eat hasish. It can be cooked with. Marijuana really is just a plant. I know that a woman would like marijuana produce. Hash is a product derived from the marijuana plant. Eating the hash could make a woman appreciate nature. The hash is made in many different ways. I beleive that the system of eye colour that is written in "THE WAY OF THE HERB" is reversed for a woman so a womans iris would match that of her man.

Marijuana notes:

It is vitally important to enjoy the correct herb for the alltitude : I would prefer to smoke a milder less resinous marijuana at a low altitude and a more resinous marijuana at a high altitude. I also prefer to smoke in the shade with some food and a juice. i do not like smoking inside a building. I do not like to drink alcohol and smoke herb together as it can cause inebreation. As I would not like to enjoy the same bottle of beer with another person. I would not like to smoke the same joint as another person. I currently smoke a blend of marijuana and tobacco but this is not ideal. Marijuana has helped to heal the very bad back. as has alcohol. I could hardly walk at one point in my life. I hardly suffer pain now

THE WORLD AND THE PEOPLE

Within the world are its people. It is as nice for me to enjoy alcohol in society as it is for me to enjoy marijuana in the natural world. Colour of alcohol is important and the wrong alcohol can cause an adverse emotional reaction in a person. As can the wrong coloured marijuana. It is also very important to appreciate that both are necessary. The world is a beautiful place but it is important to socialise with people. I have grown up with the Great British pub. it is very nice to be social with alcohol. The vocal conversation in the pub or sitting at home with freinds is as natural as thought

FRUIT OR ROOT ALCOHOL

I have witnessed that men like beer and a woman enjoy a gin and tonic. Gin is potato alcohol. It is flavoured with fruit or leaves. Beer is sometimes flavoured with a slice of lime or lemon. It is also watered down by lemonade or cordial. Root beer can be made alcoholic.I would prefer a weak alcohol such as beer at a low altitude a spirit alcohol at a high altitude and a wine in the middle. No one wants a bottle of wiskey on the beach or a crate of beer on a mountain.

ENJOY!

THE ERGONOMICS
OF COLOUR

As we all have a different physical form and the world has many different gradients and frequencies of colour. The topography of land is also suited to colour. I find walking much easier in the south of spain than I do in england. MY body is not suited to the topography. I am not as comfortable in england even though it is my place of birth. I am not the only person stuck in this situation.

WORLD CITIZENSHIP!

FUEL

I like to use a methalated spirit stove to cook. It uses purple methalated spirits. I do not like to use liquid petrolium gas or red deisel and I find their fumes toxic and I dont really understand their properties despite being the son of a car mechanic. I dont find purple methalated spirits dangerous. I do not trust myself with a gas stove. It is becoming obvious why. I also like to stare into the flame of methalated spirits burning in a copper bowl. I find it relaxing. I use a small peice of green paper for a wick to keep the flame under control and to keep the flame burning. I like to do this inside a building with a window open in the winter. Ilike the smell and it heats me and relaxes me. As colour frequency is unique so is the shape of the metal bowl used for burning fuels. I beleive that there are 6 colours of fossil fuel. to refine them and burn them in the correct place in the world is normal . I beleive that burning them in the wrong colour place in the world can cause enviromental damage due to the unique ergonomics of an enviroment. This remains to be proven by science.

I have an idea that a woman would like to see the flame of a seed oil burning in an earthware bowl of a specific shape and colour of pottery. I think that a specific type of split pine wood should be used as a wick to keep the oil burning. The seed oil should be a certain colour and could be cooked over as the fumes are much nicer for a woman to breath.

ROCKS AND STONES

I grew up in a house built of yellow sand stone, with red tiles. It is a great house. My parents built it themselves with the help of others. I like it and I appreciate its arcitecture but its just not the sort of design of building that I like to live in. I like" MEDINA "style arcitecture more. allthough I saw a picture of Tibuctoo and I did not think that the ergonomics of the city would suit my body. Arcitecture should allways follow the X. Y. Z. rule. The transference of energy should allways complete one of these three equalateral shapes. A pillar for example: should be as wide as the equalateral X shape that defines its length. If the series of equalateral X shapes are not complete then the pillar should be made wider or more narrow or the tranferance of energy will not be complete and the pillar may crumble. This same rule can be followed for a lateral beam but the energy will be transfered lateraly in an equalateral Z shape. Where the pillar meets the lateral beam would of course be an equalateral Y shape.

You can see this for yourself in modern and ancient architecture. These rules should be used in coralation with the colours of metals and stone. For example: a yellows sandstone pillar, a blue granite capping stone and a red iron lateral beam all of the correct dimensions would work well in a building in the correct part of the world. This has yet to be proven be emgineering and mathematical science.

Have fun with your engineering, building and mathematics. I beleive that I am correct and I look forward to helping to install copper lateral beams.

WEIGHT

I find aluminium to be very easy to lift but red iron is so heavy to me that I cannot lift it. I hope one day to help to engineer vehicles made of carbon fibre, copper and aluminium. As I understand the properties of them well and I beleive for example: that an aluminiun inteternal combustion engine powered by purple methalated spirit fossil fuel would work well with a copper engine head and a carbon fibre exaust manifold in a high altitude place in the world. I beleive that this place would have to be a place where purple foods grow.

THIS IS JUST AN EXAMPLE.

LANGUAGE ERGONOMICS

Excuse me if the way i write is a bit difficult to understand. It is just my method of talking and writing. I speak good spanish but I struggle to understand some spanish such as spanish from the north of spain. I would like for this writing to be seen and read by all of humanity but so far I only speak two languages well. Please feel free to translate this to your own language and to teach it. Please do not change its significance at all. Thanks.

WOOD

There are many types of tree in the natural world. I like to work with the wood of the alpine pines. I find it easy to use and I understand the woods structural properties. The yellow pine wood used in carpentry and for house building is just not a material that I am comfortale useing and it hurts me to use it.

rubber and cork also hurt plant life. We have plastics and cellulose rubber now so why harm the trees and the workers.

GASEOUS AND STILL WATER

I need to drink gaseuos mineral water from the alpine region. I feel inflated and refreshed when i drink it. I like to wash under still water but I beleive that mineral content of the water is very important as is the fuel used to heat the water. That is all that I have discovered for now but this idea can be understood and expanded by others.

SURFING AND WATERFALLS

I love to be in the sea but a lake swim would make me feel strange. I love to surf but standing under a waterfall would also make me feel strange. Are you a woman? do you feel the opposite way. I would be terrified of a night swim in a lake and I do not like to dive in the sea. The surf in fuerte Ventura and Morrocco was nice for me but I cannot surf in england due to phisical difficulties. Please expand my theory and enjoy yourselves.

WE ARE NOT OF THE WATER BUT IN THE WATER WE ARE FREE

MUSIC AND TONE

I wistle or sing when I have smoked marijuana. I drum, humb and ryme when I have alcohol in my system. One can not wistle and ryme at the same time. One can not drink and smoke at the same time. One can not silence ones vocal voice and ones mental voice at the same time. To wistle at a certain colour has a reaction to the tuning of the wistle dependent the location of the wistler on the globe and the tune itself . To sing or wistle with ones head still is to ignore the vocal range of ones voice. Physical enviroments are not flat so why not use your vocal range in harmony with them by moving ones head whilst singing or wistling.

HAVE FUN!

HOT DRINKS

I like fresh leaf (and stalk) morroccan mint tea with a small bit of brown sugar. I do not like dried leaf tea of any sort but I think that a woman would; judging by the body language of a woman when the are straining a tea bag in a cup. I have not seen any orange,purple or green coffee. The glass that I would chose for a fresh leaf (and stalk) Morrocan mint tea would be conical with one step half way up the glass. it would be green in colour and the water would be filled 3 quarters of the way up the glass to allow the steam to collect above the tea. I like to put the mint leaf(and stalk) into the glass with my hand then pour a small amount of non - refined sugar into the glass on the mint. Then pour the copper mineral water boiled in an aluminium kettle into the glass from a varied height.Then I squash the leaves a little with the sugar. I use a pine spoon of the correct colour pine tree to do this.

COLOUR LOCATION

The location of colour in realation to ones self is magnetism in its self. As I am a purple man I feel comfortable with the colour blue to my right,then green,then yellow infront of me, then orange then red in a circle. I do not do this much but I know that it helps with my magnetism and makes me feel complete. This is also true for men. For example: A blue man sat on the left of me could make me feel agitated so could a red man sat on the right of me. Especially after I have smoked marijuana,

Thanks for reading this. It has been my plesure to write this and it will be my pleasure to teach and expand this knowledge.

Robert Antill

(all I said was that this fish was definately not good enough for Jehovah)

Thanks to everyone in the world for your help and for your inspiration I am looking forward to a brighter future for all of us

Printed in the United States
by Baker & Taylor Publisher Services